EVANGELISM AND DISCIPLESHIP PLAN

SESSION 9

DR. AARON R. JONES
Foreword by Dr. Timothy M. Hill

Interfacing Evangelism and Discipleship

WORKBOOK

Evangelism and Discipleship Plan

Dr. Aaron R. Jones

Interfacing Evangelism and Discipleship – Evangelism and Discipleship Plan

Copyright © 2018 by Dr. Aaron R. Jones

Printed in the United States of America

Published by Kingdom Publishing, LLC, Odenton, MD 21113

All rights reserved. No part of this book may be reproduced or transmitted in any form or by any means, electronic or mechanical, including photocopying, recording or by any information storage and retrieval system without written permission from the author, except for the inclusion of brief quotations in a review.

All scripture quotations are from the King James Version of the Bible. Thomas Nelson Publishers, Nashville: Thomas Nelson, Inc. 1972

Editor: Sharon D. Jones

Graphic Designer: Janell McIlwain – JM Virtual Concepts

        Tiara Smith

ISBN 978-1-947741-24-9

Table of Contents

Interfacing Evangelism and Discipleship Sessions 1

Foreword 2

LEADERSHIP ROLE IN EVANGELISM AND DISCIPLESHIP

The Vision 4

The Resources 6

The Manual 8

The Intentionality 10

The Example 12

The Training 14

2 TIMOTHY 2:2 APPROACH

The Recollection 18

The Release 20

The Reproduction 22

About the Author

Contact Page

Interfacing Evangelism and Discipleship
Sessions

Session 1—**Introduction and Philosophy**

Session 2—**5 Principles to Encourage Evangelism**

Session 3—**Components of Evangelism**

Session 4—**Bait for Evangelism**

Session 5—**Methodology of Evangelism**

Session 6—**Church Planting Produces Evangelism and Discipleship**

Session 7—**Babes in Christ**

Session 8—**Components of Discipleship**

Session 9—**Evangelism and Discipleship Plan**

Session 10—**Spirit of Forgiveness**

Foreword

When God calls a man of faith and fortitude to a specific purpose in the building of His Kingdom, He uses an individual like Dr. Aaron Jones.

Feeling the urgency of the hour, Dr. Jones has shaped his participation in the FINISH Commitment by emphasizing the merging of evangelism and discipleship strategies to assist churches and individuals in their quests to effectively reach the lost. As Senior Pastor of New Hope Church of God, he is well-aware of what it takes to affect the Great Commission of our Lord.

Dr. Jones' desire is to instruct others on how to deliberately make an impact on winning souls and then discipling them for powerful Christian service. His all-inclusive approach will intrigue and provide the impetus for those willing to pursue the heart of God.

Interfacing Evangelism and Discipleship will change the course of your outreach!

Dr. Timothy M. Hill
General Overseer
Church of God, Cleveland, Tennessee

Leadership Role in Evangelism and Discipleship

The Vision

To Provide Vision

"Where there is no vision, the people perish: but he that keepeth the law, happy is he."
Proverbs 29:18

- What is your vision for Evangelism?

_____
_____
_____

- What is your vision for Discipleship?

_____
_____
_____

- What do you want your evangelism and discipleship to look like?

_____
_____
_____

The Vision

Additional Notes

❖❖❖❖❖

The Resources

To Provide Resources

"He saith unto them, How many loaves have ye? go and see. And when they knew, they say, Five, and two fishes."
Mark 6:38

- What do you have?

_____

_____

_____

- What is your budget?

_____

_____

_____

- How will you raise fund or receive donations?

_____

_____

_____

The Resources
Additional Notes

The Manual

To Provide a Manual

"And the Lord answered me, and said, Write the vision, and make it plain upon tables, that he may run that readeth it."
Habakkuk 2:2

■   What are the policies and procedures?

_____
_____
_____

■   How will the people be informed?

_____
_____
_____

■   Who can develop the manual?

_____
_____
_____

The Manual
Additional Notes

The Intentionality

To Provide Intentionality

"For I know the thoughts that I think toward you, saith the Lord, thoughts of peace, and not of evil, to give you an expected end."
Jeremiah 29:11

- How intentional are you about building God's Kingdom?

_____
_____
_____

- How will you encourage intentionality?

_____
_____
_____

- What are your steps of intention?

_____
_____
_____

The Intentionality
Additional Notes

The Example

To Provide an Example

"Be ye followers of me, even as I also am of Christ."
I Corinthians 11:1

■ Jesus was the example of Evangelism and Discipleship.

_____

_____

_____

■ A title or position doesn't remove the responsibility of evangelizing and discipling.

_____

_____

_____

■ Evangelism and disciple may take different forms as you move in ministry.

_____

_____

_____

The Example
Additional Notes

The Training

To Provide Training

"But the Comforter, which is the Holy Ghost, whom the Father will send in my name, he shall teach you all things, and bring all things to your remembrance, whatsoever I have said unto you."
John 14:26

- Jesus trained His disciples.

_____
_____
_____

- Someone must be a teacher, and someone must be the student.

_____
_____
_____

- Training provides a continuum of evangelism and discipleship.

_____
_____
_____

Additional Notes

2 Timothy 2:2 Approach

"And the things that thou hast heard of me among many witnesses, the same commit thou to faithful men, who shall be able to teach others also."

The Recollection

- **The Recollection**

"And the *<u>things that thou hast heard of me</u>* among many witnesses…"

_____
_____
_____
_____
_____
_____
_____

Additional Notes

The Release

■ **The Release**

"…the same *commit thou* to faithful men…"

_____
_____
_____
_____
_____
_____
_____

The Release

Additional Notes

The Reproduction

- **The Reproduction**

"…who shall be able to *teach others* also."

The Reproduction

Additional Notes

About the Author

DR. AARON R. JONES serves as Senior Pastor of New Hope Church of God. Under his pastorate is New Hope Kiddie Kollege, Inc (Daycare) and New Hope Community Outreach Services, Inc. Dr. Jones also oversees New Hope Church of God Ghana (2 churches) and New Hope Church of God Uganda (3 churches).

Dr. Jones is an Ordained Bishop with the Church of God denomination and is the DELMARVA-DC District Overseer (16 churches). Dr. Jones serves on DELMARVA-DC's Regional Council, Ministerial Internship Program Board, Urban Ministry Committee, Finance Committee, and Chaplain's Board. He also serves on both the Church of God's International and DELMARVA-DC Ministry to the Military Board. In his local community, Dr. Jones serves as a Chaplain for the Charles County Sheriff Department. He also serves as Board Secretary for the United Ministers Coalition of Southern Maryland, Inc.

Being obedient to 2 Timothy 2:15, "Study to show thyself approved…," Dr. Jones received a Doctorate in Theology and Pastoral Counseling from Life

Christian University and a Doctorate in Christian Counseling from American Christian College and Seminary. He is a certified Pastoral Counselor with the International Association of Christian Counseling Professionals. He is a Life and Pastoral Coach. He is the former Executive Vice President of the National Bible College and Seminary in Fort Washington, Maryland.

Dr. Jones has published ten books and a soul-wining project that provide a biblical foundation for Christian doctrine and discipline. He has recorded a CD entitled, Peace in the Storm. He is the founder and owner of God's Comfort Ministries, LLC, which provides Christian literature, evangelism training, and spiritual guidance. He has appeared live on TCT Network; WATC-TV's Atlanta Live; Babbie's House (hosted by CCM artist Babbie Mason); and In Concert Today on DCTV. He has done radio interviews with Radio One's WYCB's program; The Praise Fest Show; and online with Total Prayze. He was featured on the cover of Change Gospel Magazine and interviewed on Promoting Purpose Magazine.

Dr. Jones not only serves God, but his country as well. He has served over 20 years in the Armed Forces. He is a retired Chaplain with the Army National Guard. He participated in both Operation Noble Eagle (2003) and Operation Iraqi Freedom III (2005).

Dr. Jones is happily married to the former Sharon Russell. He sincerely believes without her love, support, and encouragement, many of his goals would not have been accomplished.

Contact Page

Mailing Address:

150 Post Office Road #1079

Waldorf, Maryland 20604

Website: www.godscomfort.net

Email: drjones@godscomfortmin.net

Facebook: God's Comfort Ministries

Twitter: @GodsComfort_Min

Instagram: @godscomfort_min

GOD'S COMFORT MINISTRIES

God's Comfort Ministries (GCM) provides practical Christian books, teachings, trainings, and coaching to new converts and seasoned believers. GCM provides understanding of the doctrinal principles of the Bible.

Services Provided

Pastoral and Life Coaching

Evangelism and Discipleship Training

Spiritual Guidance

New Author Consultation

Christian Literature

www.ingramcontent.com/pod-product-compliance
Lightning Source LLC
Chambersburg PA
CBHW081358080526
44588CB00016B/2533